Weird Insects

MICHAEL WOREK

FIREFLY BOOKS

A FIREFLY BOOK

Published by Firefly Books Ltd. 2013

Copyright © 2013 Firefly Books Ltd.

Text copyright © 2013 Michael Worek

First printing

Publisher Cataloging-in-Publication Data (U.S.)

Worek, Michael.
    Weird insects / Michael Worek.
[64] p. : col. photos. ; cm.
Includes index.
Summary: A beautifully illustrated guide to some of the most weird and wonderful insects of the world.
ISBN-13: 978-1-77085-235-8
ISBN-13: 978-1-77085-234-1 (pbk.)
1. Insects -- Juvenile literature. I. Title.
595.7 dc23   QL467.2.M377   2013

Library and Archives Canada Cataloguing in Publication

Worek, Michael
    Weird insects / Michael Worek.
Includes index.
ISBN 978-1-77085-235-8 (bound).
ISBN 978-1-77085-234-1 (pbk.)
    1. Insects--Juvenile literature. I. Title.
QL467.2.M388 2013   j595.7   C2013-901247-8

All images are copyright Nature Picture Library, jointly with the following photographers:
page 4, cover © Chris Mattison; page 5 © Kim Taylor; page 6 © Alex Hyde; page 7 © Kim Taylor; page 8 © MYN / Niall Benvie; page 9 © Chris Mattison; page 10 © MYN / Seth Patterson; page 11 © MYN / Niall Benvie; page 12 © Alex Hyde; page 13 © Chris Mattison; page 14, back cover top right © ARCO; page 15 © John Abbott; page 16 © Kim Taylor; page 17 © Kim Taylor; page 18 © MYN / Clay Bolt; page 19 © Chris Mattison; page 20 © John Abbott; page 21 © Nature Production; page 22 © Alex Hyde; page 23 © MYN / Clay Bolt; page 24 © MYN / Marko Masterl; page 25 © Chris Mattison; page 26 © Kim Taylor; page 27 © MYN / Niall Benvie; page 28 © Nick Garbutt; page 29 © ARCO; page 30 © Kim Taylor; page 31 © Mark Bowler; page 32 © MYN / Mac Stone; page 33 © Kim Taylor; page 34 © MYN / Seth Patterson; page 35 © Chris Mattison; page 36 © MYN / John Tiddy; page 37 © John Abbott; page 38 © Alex Hyde; page 39 © Chris Mattison; page 40 © MYN / Joris van Alphen; page 41 © Chris Mattison; page 42 © Alex Hyde; page 43 © MYN / Piotr Naskrecki; page 44–45 © Alex Hyde; page 46 © Alex Hyde; page 47 © MYN / Piotr Naskrecki; page 48 © Alex Hyde; page 49 © Alex Hyde; page 50–51 © Kim Taylor; page 52 © Alex Hyde; page 53 © Alex Hyde; page 54 © MYN / Paul Harcourt Davies; page 55 © Wild Wonders of Europe / Benvie; page 56 © Alex Hyde; page 57 © MYN / Brady Beck; page 58 © Alex Hyde; page 59, back cover bottom left © Chris Mattison; page 60 © John Abbott; page 61 © Kim Taylor; page 62 © Kim Taylor; page 63 © Kim Taylor.

Published in the United States by
Firefly Books (U.S.) Inc.
P.O. Box 1338, Ellicott Station
Buffalo, New York 14205

Published in Canada by
Firefly Books Ltd.
50 Staples Avenue, Unit 1
Richmond Hill, Ontario L4B 0A7

Cover and interior design by Jacqueline Hope Raynor
Printed in China

The publisher gratefully acknowledges the financial support for our publishing program by the Government of Canada through the Canada Book Fund as administered by the Department of Canadian Heritage.

INTRODUCTION

There are more insects than any other kind of living thing in the world. There are so many that if you could count all the species of living things in the world, well over one million of them would be insects. In addition to being numerous, insects are endlessly fascinating and varied – and, to us, sometimes, weird. Most of the really colorful and weird looking insects live in the warmest lands that lie around the equator, but interesting insects can be found just about anywhere in the world.

An insect is often defined as an organism with three pairs of legs and three body regions: the first is the head, the second is the thorax and the third is the abdomen. Insects also have a pair of antennae and external mouthparts.

The head contains the antennae, mouth and eyes. Some insects drink nectar, and have mouthparts modified into a tube, called a proboscis, to suck up liquid. Other insects have mouthparts that allow them to chew. The pair of antennae is used to perceive sounds, smells and vibrations. Insects can have compound eyes that are usually large with many lenses that let it see all around or they can have a simple eye that contains just a single lens. Most insects have both kinds of eyes.

The middle of the insect's body, called the thorax, includes the legs and the wings. All insect legs have five parts and are adapted to let it move efficiently in its habitat. Wings are found in many different shapes and sizes, and are adapted to the insect's special needs. The last section of the insect's body, called the abdomen, contains the stomach, intestines, sexual organs and glands that secrete a scent for marking the insect's territory or attracting a mate.

The insects in the book represent just a tiny fraction of the range and diversity of what we already know exists. But even this tiny sample is enough to suggest the riches that await anyone who takes the time to observe the insects around them.

MACLEAY'S SPECTRE

Extatosoma tiaratum

This huge stick insect is originally from Australia but it is now kept as a pet all over the world. Females, like the one shown here, are covered with small spike-like thorns for defense and can grow to 20 centimeters (8 inches) long. Only the males can fly and they blend in with the foliage for protection. Eggs can take up to four months to hatch; the female flicks them to the ground with her tail after she lays them.

HAZELNUT WEEVIL

Curculio nucum

This little weevil is called a "hazelnut" weevil because it lays its eggs inside a hazelnut. Its long snout ends in a pair of strong jaws that allow the female weevil to drill a hole in the hard outer shell of the nut. Once the hole is drilled, the female puts an egg in the hole. When the egg hatches, the larva eats the inside of the nut.

ROSEMARY BEETLE

Chrysolina americana

This beautiful blue and orange-striped metallic beetle got its name because it is so often found on rosemary plants. Rosemary is used as a seasoning in many of our recipes and this beetle likes it too. It is such a fussy eater that it only feeds on the leaves of three plants: rosemary, lavender and thyme. Rosemary beetles are found only in Europe although its Latin name is *Chrysolina americana* because when the beetle was first identified it was mistakenly thought to come from America.

CASE-MAKING LEAF BEETLE

Cryptocephalus sp.

This adult case-making leaf beetle lives on a diet of leaves. When the female lays her eggs, she wraps each one in a hard cigar-shaped case made from dried feces for protection from predators. When the egg hatches, the larva makes a small hole in the case just large enough so it can feed. As the larva grows, it adds feces to the case to make it larger. The larva can remain in the case for up to two years.

ORANGE LADYBIRD

Halyzia sedecimguttata

Most of the ladybird beetles we see are red with black spots and eat aphids and other small, soft-bodied insects. But members of the lady beetle family (Coccinellidae) come in all sizes, colors and eating habits. This orange ladybird feeds on mildew (a powder-like fungus). They usually have 16 white spots on their back and are found throughout Europe and the United Kingdom.

WEEVIL

Curculionidae

Weevils are beetles that have long snouts. They have small jaws, called mandibles, that can be used to chew holes in nuts, stems and other parts of plants that the weevil uses for food. Some, like the boll weevil that eats cotton plants, can cause great damage. Most weevil larvae burrow inside plants but some burrow into the ground and attack plant roots for food.

ANACUA TORTOISE BEETLE

Coptocycla texana

Tortoise beetles are named for their broad, expanded shell. When disturbed, these beetles can hunker down under the shell with the head, antennae and legs completely covered. Many tortoise beetles are brilliantly metallic in life, some species can even change color from orange to gold, but their colors fade quickly after they die. The anacua tortoise beetle occurs in the southwestern United States although its relatives are found mostly in South and Central America.

THISTLE TORTOISE BEETLE

Cassida rubiginosa

The tortoise beetle does look a little like a tortoise, with its metallic green body and legs sticking out from underneath. These insects feed on the surface of leaves. They spend the winter under tree bark or leaf litter and emerge in the spring to feed and mate. The larvae have a flattened body with spines all around and protect themselves from predators by coating their tail with excrement and holding it over their body like an umbrella.

MINSTREL BUG

Graphosoma lineatum

This brightly colored minstrel bug belongs to a group of stinkbugs sometimes called terrestrial turtle bugs because of their turtle-like backs. They have a beak resembling a drinking straw, which they use to suck the sap out of foul-tasting plants. Hence, minstrel bugs taste and even smell bad. Their bright colors warn potential enemies to stay away from them. They prefer warm climates and are found in Italy and throughout southern Europe.

SHIELD BUG

Pygoplatus sp.

This giant shield bug from Southeast Asia has two sharp spikes behind its head for protection against predators. It also has glands that contain stinky and painful defensive chemicals that it can spray when frightened. They are known for the care they take of the young. The mother guards her eggs, then carries the babies beneath her belly until they are strong enough to fend for themselves.

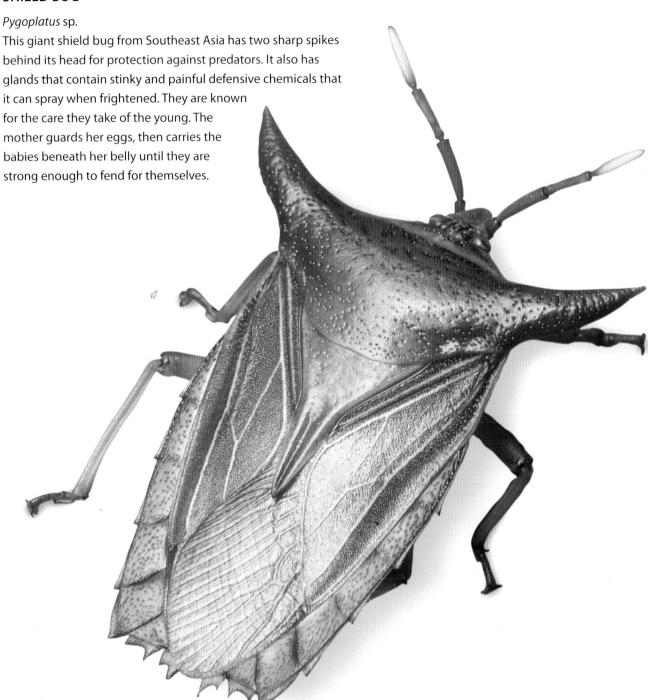

DEAD-NETTLE LEAF BEETLE

Chrysolina fastuosa

This beautiful metallic green and orange leaf beetle with long antennae only feeds on certain types of plants, including some noxious weeds. Scientists are studying ways of using it for biological control of weeds. The beetle's name comes from the fact that it is often found on the dead-nettle plant where it eats the flower heads. The dead-nettle plant looks like it has sharp spikes that would sting, but in fact the spikes are soft and the plant does not sting – hence the name "dead" nettle.

RAINBOW SCARAB

Phanaeus difformis

Beetles in the genus *Phanaeus* are often called rainbow scarabs because of their many beautiful colors. Only the male beetle has the large horn on the head. The beetle in this photograph is sitting with its antennae extended to "sniff" for food. These are dung-rolling beetles that develop in the excrement of other animals. Mated pairs cooperate to dig burrows and bury balls of animal excrement that serve as food for the larvae that will hatch from the eggs they lay in the dung-stacked nest.

RAINBOW SHIELD BUG

Calidea dregii

Shield-backed bugs, like the rainbow shield bug shown on this page, have glands between the first and second pair of legs that produce a foul-smelling liquid that keeps predators away. They have a "shield" (properly called a "scutellum") that is a hard outer shell, covering their entire back. It is an African species of a group of shield-backed bugs known as the "blue bugs" because of their metallic blue sheen.

BRASSICA BUG

Eurydema oleracea

This brassica bug is a stink bug that is found in Europe and feeds on cabbage and related plants. It uses its piercing mouthparts to suck juices from developing seeds and other parts of the plant. Stink bugs have long antennae with five segments and a well-designed hard outer shell that provides protection. They are found world-wide. Although they are regarded as pests because they feed on a variety of crops that humans grow for food, some are beneficial to humans because they eat other insect pests.

STINK BUG NYMPHS

Pentatomidae
The bright colors of these stink bug nymphs are a signal to predators that they have a foul taste. Because these stink bugs are still in the nymph form, their wings are undeveloped and visible here only as small flaps that leave most of the top of the abdomen exposed. The black patches you can see on the abdomen are the stink glands. The young remain in the nymph stage for several weeks before becoming fully grown adults. The female stink bug lays eggs two or three times a year.

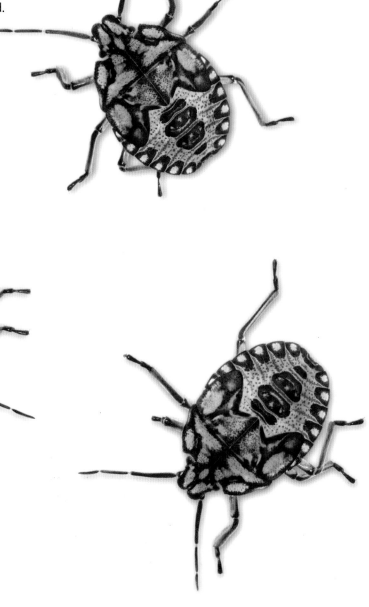

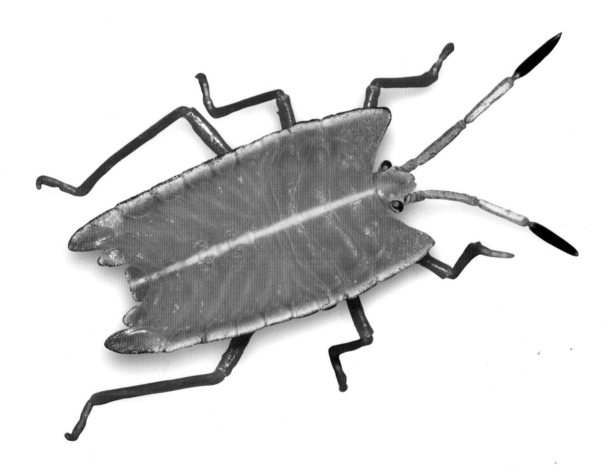

PINK STINK BUG

Pycanum rubens

This is the nymph stage of the pink stink bug. When it matures, it will change its color from pink to green and grow two pairs of large wings. Pink is a fairly rare color for insects since it makes the insect easy to spot when it sits on a green plant. In this case, the color acts as a warning to predators because, as the name suggests, the chemicals in its body smell awful when the insect is crushed or eaten by a predator.

EASTERN RHINOCEROS BEETLE

Dynastes tityus

This huge male eastern rhinoceros beetle is thought to be the strongest animal on Earth in proportion to its size. It can lift over 800 times its own weight and is the heaviest insect in North America. Only the males have the horns, which they use to fight with rival males to secure desirable territories. Rhinoceros beetles can remain in the larval stage for up to 2 years. After they emerge as an adult, they only live for about 6 months.

JAPANESE RHINOCEROS BEETLE

Allomyrina dichotoma

This heavily armored rhinoceros beetle normally has its hind wings concealed under hard, protective front wings. When it opens its front wings, as in this picture, the delicate hind wings can be unfolded and used to fly. They are very popular in Japan and are sold as pets. They spend most of their life underground and only emerge as fully grown beetles for about four months when they mate. The large horns are used by the male to fight other males during the mating season.

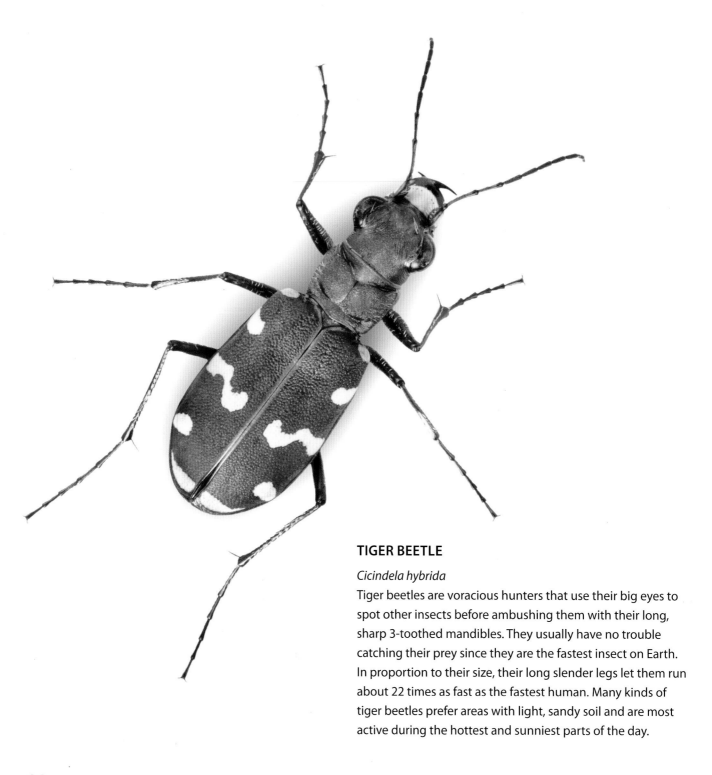

TIGER BEETLE

Cicindela hybrida

Tiger beetles are voracious hunters that use their big eyes to spot other insects before ambushing them with their long, sharp 3-toothed mandibles. They usually have no trouble catching their prey since they are the fastest insect on Earth. In proportion to their size, their long slender legs let them run about 22 times as fast as the fastest human. Many kinds of tiger beetles prefer areas with light, sandy soil and are most active during the hottest and sunniest parts of the day.

SIX-SPOTTED TIGER BEETLE

Cicindela sexguttata
This six-spotted tiger beetle lives alone during most of the year, only coming together to breed. The female deposits an egg in a hole in the ground and covers it with dirt. When the eggs hatch, the larvae burrow down into the ground and stay in the burrow for as long as a year, sticking their heads out to catch food. The adults hunt during the day. At night they return to the same burrow in which they were born.

SCOPOLI'S WEEVIL

Otiorhynchus gemmatus

This European weevil is a flightless member of a group called the broad-nosed weevils. Its black body is covered with elongated, hair-like scales that produce the mottled appearance with reddish-brown legs. Scopoli's weevil larvae feed on plant roots while the adults chew small holes in the leaves and flowers of trees. The adults are very tough and well protected with their wing covers fused into a virtually indestructible capsule for protection against its enemies.

GIRAFFE-NECKED WEEVIL

Trachelophorus giraffa
Giraffe-necked weevils get their name
from their extended neck. The neck of the
male, like the one shown here, can be two
to three times as long as the neck of the
female and is used to fight off other males
during breeding season. They are also called
leaf-rolling weevils because of the female's
remarkable habit of rolling up a leaf and
depositing an egg inside the roll. The beetle
lives only on the island of Madagascar.

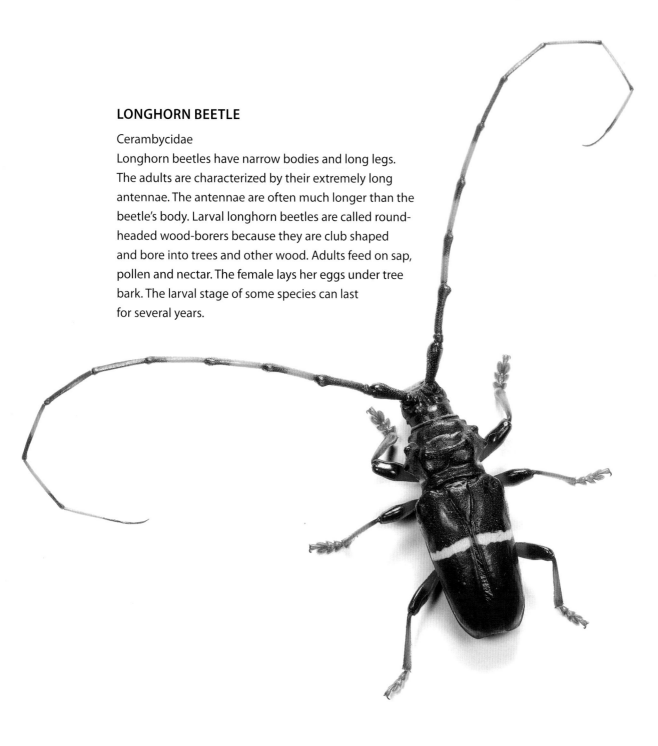

LONGHORN BEETLE

Cerambycidae

Longhorn beetles have narrow bodies and long legs. The adults are characterized by their extremely long antennae. The antennae are often much longer than the beetle's body. Larval longhorn beetles are called round-headed wood-borers because they are club shaped and bore into trees and other wood. Adults feed on sap, pollen and nectar. The female lays her eggs under tree bark. The larval stage of some species can last for several years.

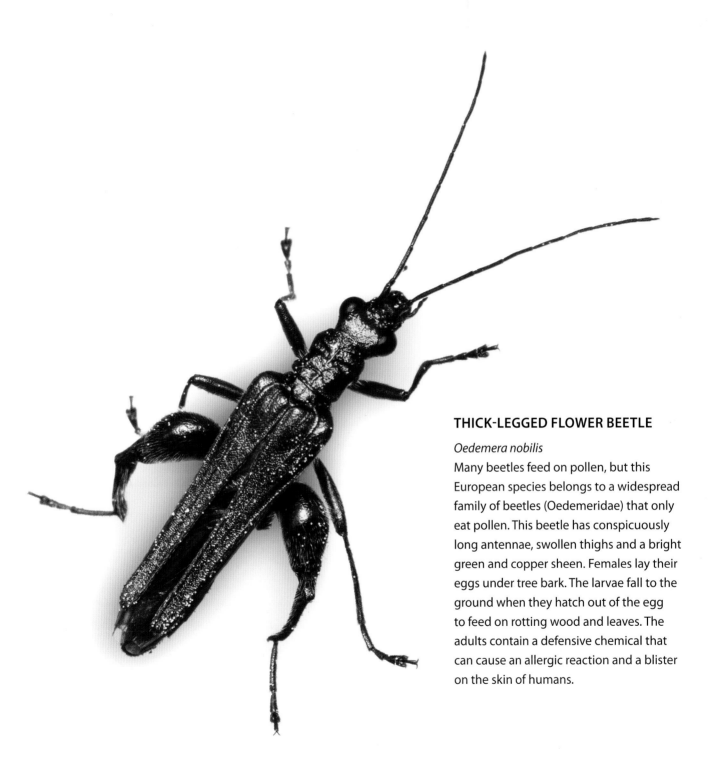

THICK-LEGGED FLOWER BEETLE

Oedemera nobilis
Many beetles feed on pollen, but this European species belongs to a widespread family of beetles (Oedemeridae) that only eat pollen. This beetle has conspicuously long antennae, swollen thighs and a bright green and copper sheen. Females lay their eggs under tree bark. The larvae fall to the ground when they hatch out of the egg to feed on rotting wood and leaves. The adults contain a defensive chemical that can cause an allergic reaction and a blister on the skin of humans.

VIOLIN BEETLE

Mormolyce phyllodes

This oddly flattened beetle with a small head is called a violin beetle because its shape resembles a violin. The huge wing case is much larger than the actual body. The flat shape is an adaptation that allows the beetle to live between the layers of bracket fungi which look like stacks of flat mushrooms growing on dead trees and rotting logs. The beetle can spray an acid that immobilizes its victim.

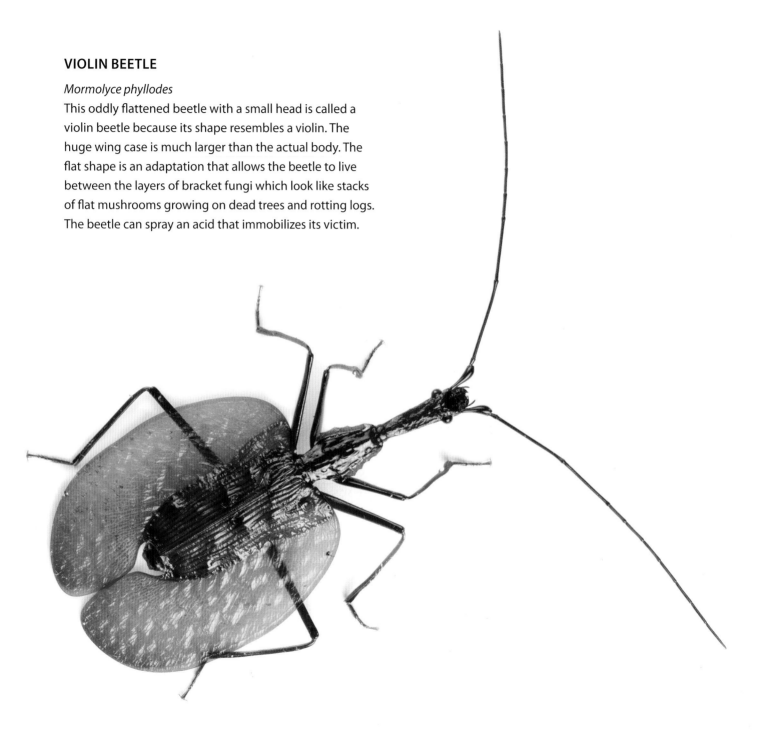

FIREBUG

Pyrrhocoris apterus
Firebugs have distinctive black and red coloring. Although native to Europe, these conspicuous true bugs were recently accidentally introduced to North America. The female firebug lays eggs that hatch in 10 to 14 days. The nymph stages last for another two to three weeks before the insect matures. As a defense, firebugs can emit a foul odor from the scent glands on either side of the body. Like other true bugs, they feed using a straw-like beak.

BULLDOG ANT

Myrmecia sp.

Australian bulldog ants are among the most aggressive of all ants. They have a combination of good vision, mean temper, large size and a really potent sting. They get the name bulldog from their strong grip and savage bite. They can be dangerous to those allergic to insect stings and have been known to cause death in humans. Almost all of the 90 known species live in Australia. The larvae eat small insects provided by the adults. Mature insects eat mostly honeydew, seeds, fruit and plant nectar.

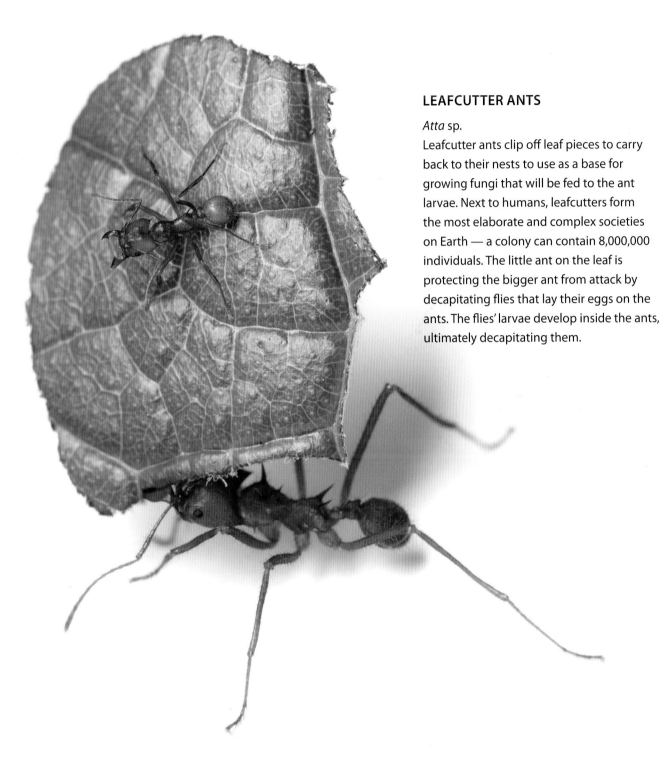

LEAFCUTTER ANTS

Atta sp.

Leafcutter ants clip off leaf pieces to carry back to their nests to use as a base for growing fungi that will be fed to the ant larvae. Next to humans, leafcutters form the most elaborate and complex societies on Earth — a colony can contain 8,000,000 individuals. The little ant on the leaf is protecting the bigger ant from attack by decapitating flies that lay their eggs on the ants. The flies' larvae develop inside the ants, ultimately decapitating them.

RED VELVET ANT

Dasymutilla occidentalis

Despite the name, velvet ants are wasps, not ants. They are called "velvet" ants because of the smooth, dense covering of red and black hair. This female is tough-skinned and carries her own very powerful sting, from which it gets the alternate name "cow killer" since the sting seems powerful enough to kill a cow. The female deposits eggs inside the ground nest of a bee or wasp. The eggs hatch quickly and eat the eggs of the bee or wasp.

SOLITARY WASP

Vespidae

The skinny, partially folded wings of this wasp mark it as a member of the same family as the social paper wasps. However, this species is a solitary wasp that makes a pottery-like mud nest and stocks it with paralyzed caterpillars to serve as food for its larvae. When they are not hunting for caterpillars, solitary wasps spend a lot of time grooming themselves and sipping nectar from flowers.

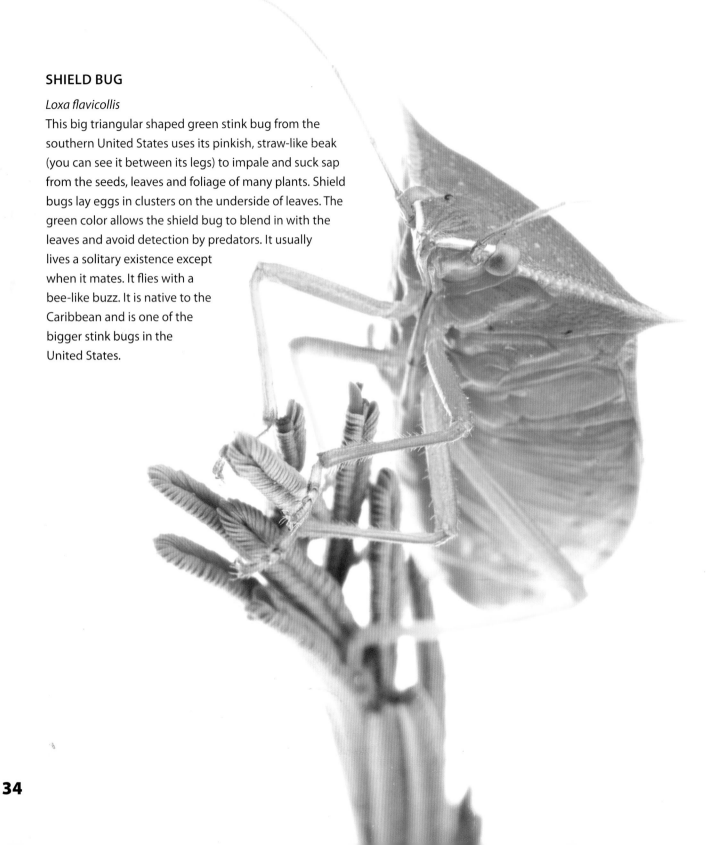

SHIELD BUG

Loxa flavicollis

This big triangular shaped green stink bug from the
southern United States uses its pinkish, straw-like beak
(you can see it between its legs) to impale and suck sap
from the seeds, leaves and foliage of many plants. Shield
bugs lay eggs in clusters on the underside of leaves. The
green color allows the shield bug to blend in with the
leaves and avoid detection by predators. It usually
lives a solitary existence except
when it mates. It flies with a
bee-like buzz. It is native to the
Caribbean and is one of the
bigger stink bugs in the
United States.

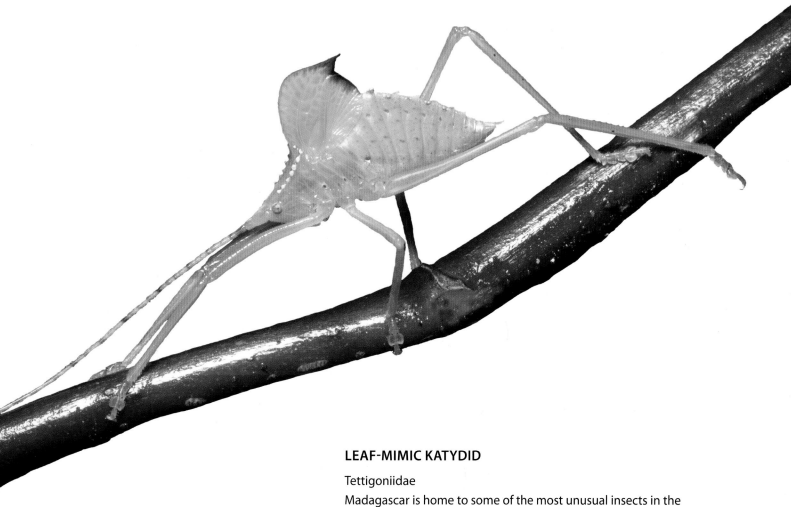

LEAF-MIMIC KATYDID

Tettigoniidae

Madagascar is home to some of the most unusual insects in the world. This long-horned grasshopper is one of those that occur nowhere else in the world, but similar leaf-mimics in the katydid family are found almost everywhere. Their color and shape allow them to use camouflage to survive. Some look exactly like a leaf and the edges of the body can even have the appearance of bite marks. When they move, they rock back and forth as if they are a leaf blowing in the wind.

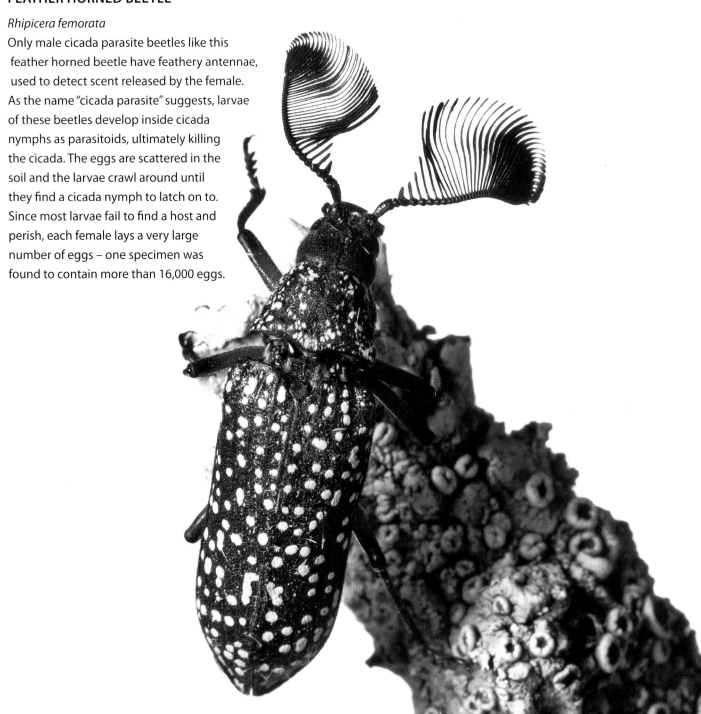

FEATHER HORNED BEETLE

Rhipicera femorata

Only male cicada parasite beetles like this feather horned beetle have feathery antennae, used to detect scent released by the female. As the name "cicada parasite" suggests, larvae of these beetles develop inside cicada nymphs as parasitoids, ultimately killing the cicada. The eggs are scattered in the soil and the larvae crawl around until they find a cicada nymph to latch on to. Since most larvae fail to find a host and perish, each female lays a very large number of eggs – one specimen was found to contain more than 16,000 eggs.

IRONCLAD BEETLE

Zopherus nodulosus haldemani

Ironclad beetles probably have the toughest armor of any insect. The armor not only protects them from predators but also from losing moisture. Many live in desert regions. Most ironclad beetles are found under bark and rotting wood. Despite its tough hide, when disturbed or frightened, they tuck their legs in and fall to the ground and play dead. They are very slow moving and can't fly. They live a very long time for an insect, some have survived up to seven years in captivity.

SPINY FLOWER MANTIS

Pseudocreobotra wahlbergii

Many insects that spend time exposed on flowers are either camouflaged to be invisible to their enemies or brightly colored to suggest to predators that they are poisonous or taste foul, but this spiny flower mantid seems to be deterring potential predators by imitating an eye of a dangerous vertebrate. Also, the bands and stripes break up the shape of the mantid, making it less recognizable as a potential food item. Mantids are themselves predators, snatching other flower visitors with their spiky front legs.

LANTERNFLY

Pyrops sp.

Some of the larger planthoppers like this peanut-headed insect are misnamed "lanternflies" because they were once thought to produce light. There are many kinds of bioluminescent insects, but planthoppers are not among them. The long, peanut shaped protrusion from the head is mostly hollow and can sometimes be nearly as long as the insect's body. Many have flashier hind wings that they spread when frightened, often revealing polka-dots or eye spots to startle would-be predators. All planthoppers suck sap out of plants and are harmless to people.

GIANT CICADA

Tacua speciosa

This giant Southeast Asian cicada is one of the largest cicadas. Its wings have conspicuous veins and can span almost five inches. Most cicadas stay underground for several years as nymphs living on the sap from roots before emerging as a short-lived winged adult. Cicadas in the North American genus *Magicicada* live for 13 to 17 years as underground nymphs, but once they emerge as adults they only live for a few weeks.

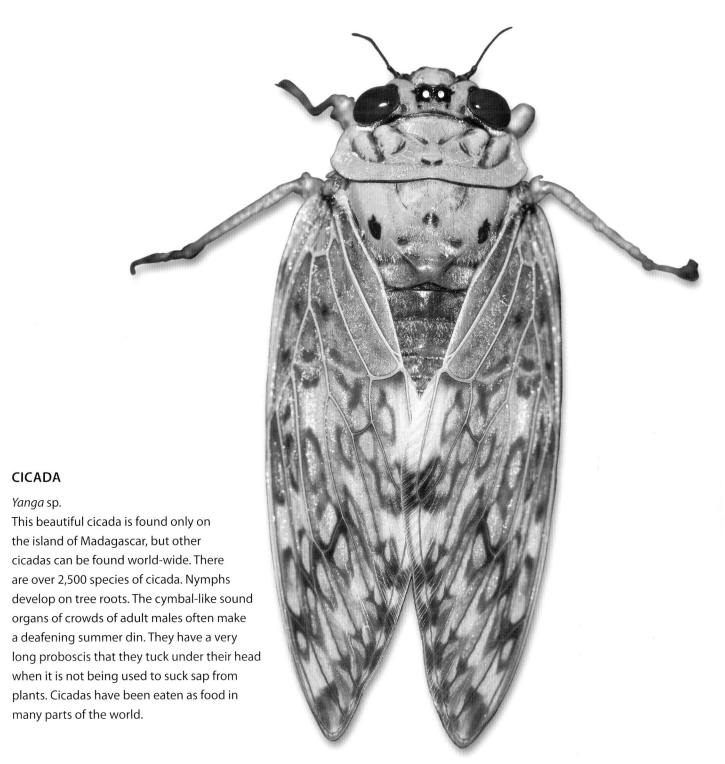

CICADA

Yanga sp.

This beautiful cicada is found only on the island of Madagascar, but other cicadas can be found world-wide. There are over 2,500 species of cicada. Nymphs develop on tree roots. The cymbal-like sound organs of crowds of adult males often make a deafening summer din. They have a very long proboscis that they tuck under their head when it is not being used to suck sap from plants. Cicadas have been eaten as food in many parts of the world.

FIELD GRASSHOPPER

Chorthippus brunneus

Most insects are either green or brown in color because they rely on camouflage to hide from predators. Several species of insects do produce pink individuals on rare occasions, including some katydids and a few grasshoppers, but we are not sure why. This is a pink nymph of a common short-horned grasshopper. As the name suggests, they are often found in fields where they chew on different kinds of grass.

GREEN KATYDID

Tettigoniidae

This katydid is a young nymph that has not yet grown visible wings. Katydids are related to crickets and, like crickets, usually develop into adults with fully developed wings that are rubbed against one another to sing. Katydids call to each other at night. Each species makes its own distinctive song, from tunes to trills to ticks.

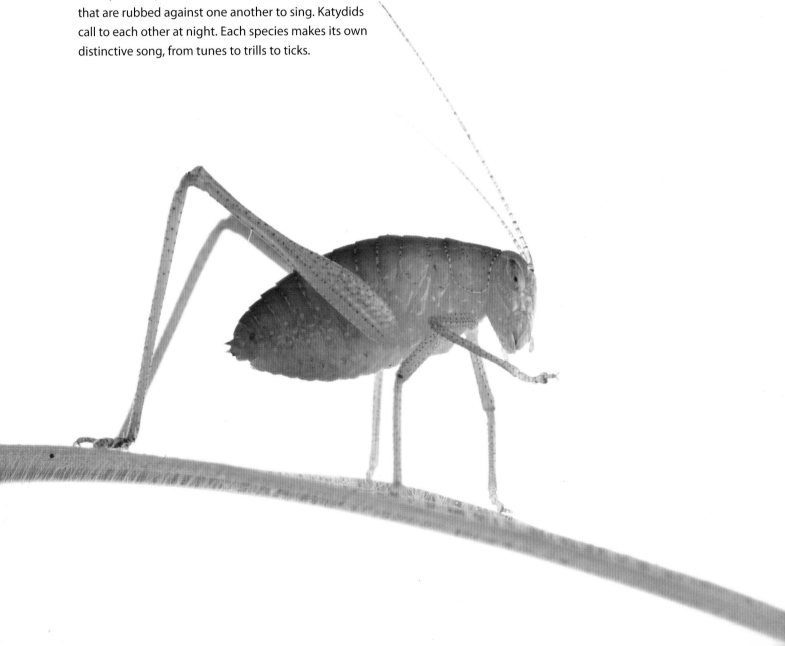

WIDE-ARMED MANTID

Cilnia humeralis

This wide-armed mantid is native to Africa but it is one of many mantis species now sold as a pet in many parts of the world. Like other mantids, it is a voracious predator and will eat just about any insect or spider it can catch, including other wide-armed mantids. Mantids are ambush predators, they sit motionless until they spot prey with their big eyes, then they spring forward to grasp it with their spiked front legs.

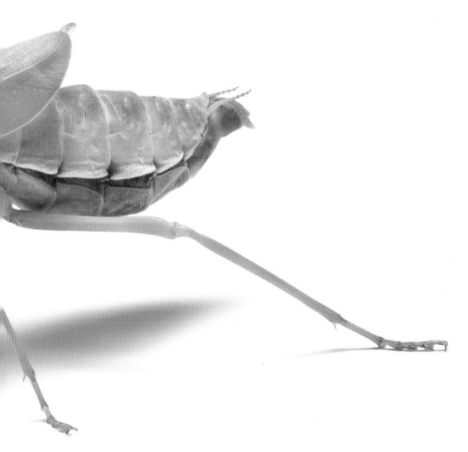

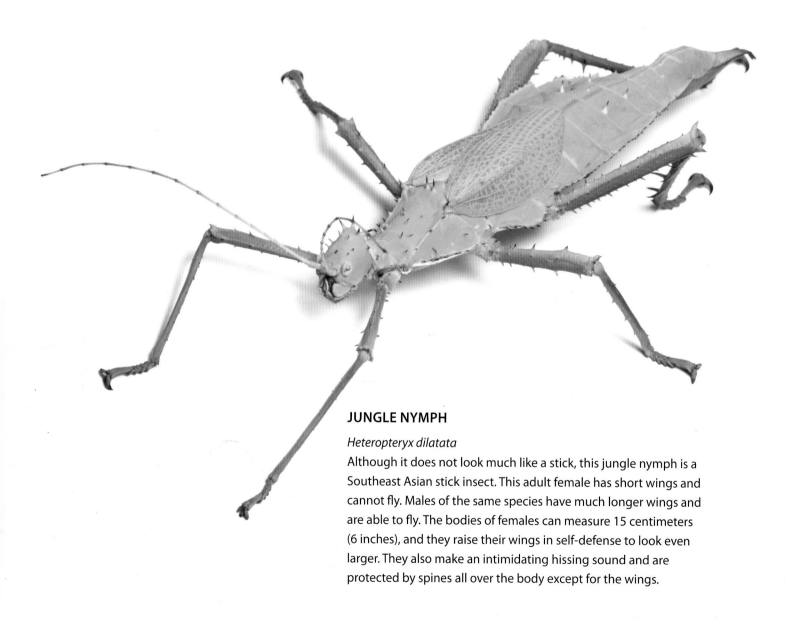

JUNGLE NYMPH

Heteropteryx dilatata
Although it does not look much like a stick, this jungle nymph is a Southeast Asian stick insect. This adult female has short wings and cannot fly. Males of the same species have much longer wings and are able to fly. The bodies of females can measure 15 centimeters (6 inches), and they raise their wings in self-defense to look even larger. They also make an intimidating hissing sound and are protected by spines all over the body except for the wings.

TREEHOPPER

Ophiderma sp.

Treehoppers are plant-sucking bugs with an armor-like shield extending from the head right back over the abdomen. In some species this shield provides protection from predators and in other species, it just provides camouflage. Treehoppers come in lots of strange shapes, some resembling ants. Treehoppers produce a sugary fluid called honeydew that is very attractive to ants, which protect them in return for the fluid.

SOCIAL WASP

Vespidae

This worker wasp looks like she is feeding something to the larvae living in the cells or chambers in her nest. She has folded her wings lengthwise under her body so they are barely visible in this photograph. Most members of this family (Vespidae) are social, living together and cooperatively tending their young in paper nests made of chewed wood fiber, which the workers make from tree bark.

RUBY-TAILED WASP

Chrysis ignita

Ruby-tailed wasps belong to a family of jewel-like wasps that have lost their stings but have very hard bodies. To defend themselves when threatened, they roll up into an impenetrable ball covering all their legs and wings. They invade the nests of stinging wasps, where they lay their eggs.

STINGING CATERPILLAR

Saturniidae

A staggering diversity of caterpillars like this one live in Central America. Many of them are brightly colored and covered by long spines. The bright colors are a warning to predators — and people — to stay away. Many species have hollow, poison-filled spines that really hurt when they break off under the skin. This defends the caterpillars against large predators, however they are still vulnerable to small ants and parasitic wasps.

DEATH'S HEAD CATERPILLAR

Acherontia actropos
The prominent tail on this caterpillar makes it easy to identify.
Adults have markings on the thorax that look remarkably
like a skull and give the species its common name
"death's head hawk moth." This very large moth
is found in Europe and Africa. Its favorite food
plants are members of the potato family.

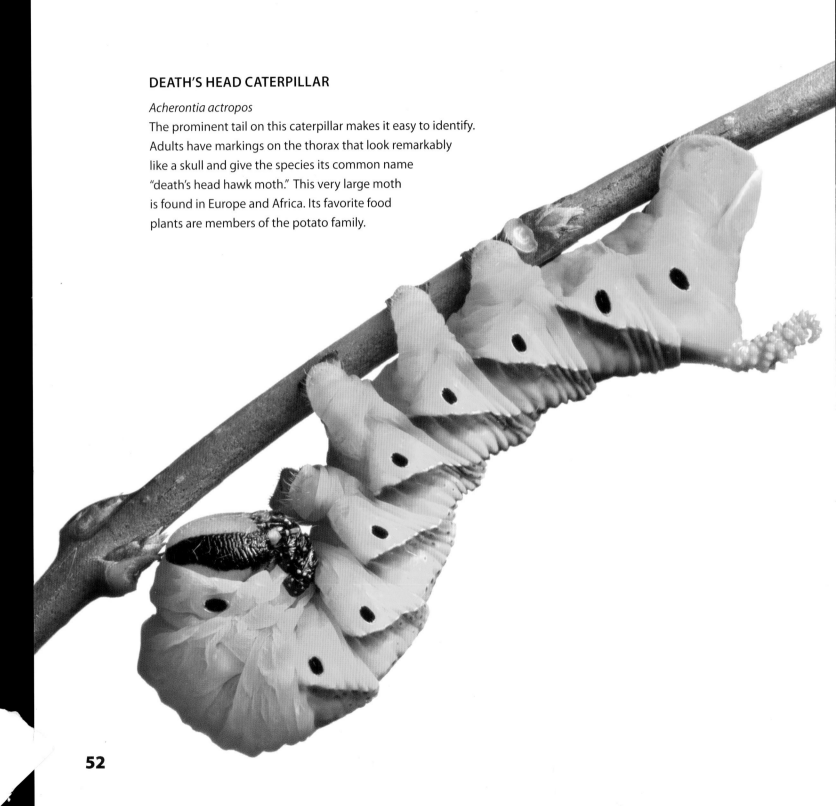

ELEPHANT HAWKMOTH CATERPILLAR

Deilephila elpenor
You can identify this massive elephant hawk moth caterpillar by the distinctive pointy tail and the startling eyespots on the top of the thorax. Its head is small, almost hidden at the front of the body at the bottom of the picture. This European species will eventually turn into a pretty green and pink moth. Hawk moths get their name because they are streamlined and fast flyers; they look a bit like tiny jet planes.

53

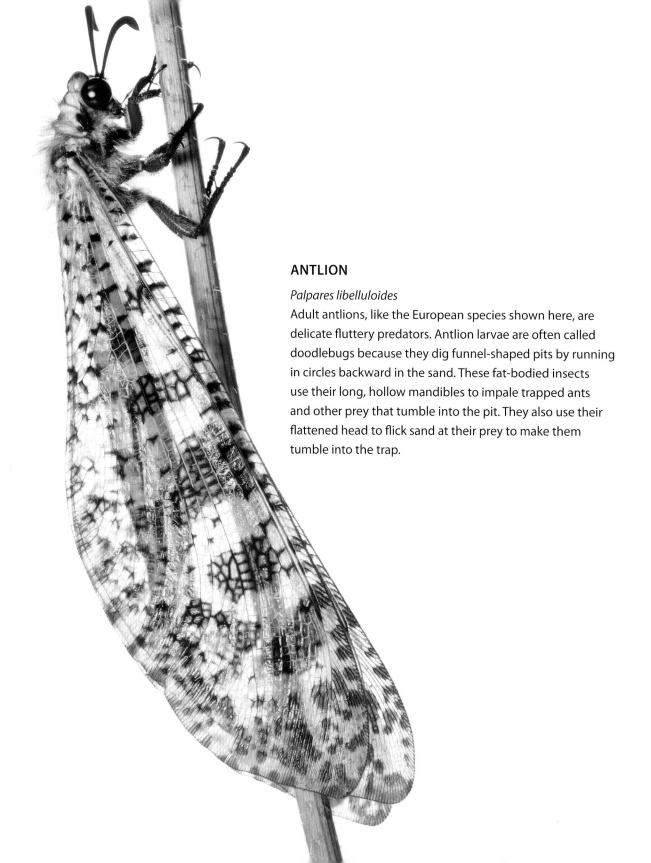

ANTLION

Palpares libelluloides

Adult antlions, like the European species shown here, are delicate fluttery predators. Antlion larvae are often called doodlebugs because they dig funnel-shaped pits by running in circles backward in the sand. These fat-bodied insects use their long, hollow mandibles to impale trapped ants and other prey that tumble into the pit. They also use their flattened head to flick sand at their prey to make them tumble into the trap.

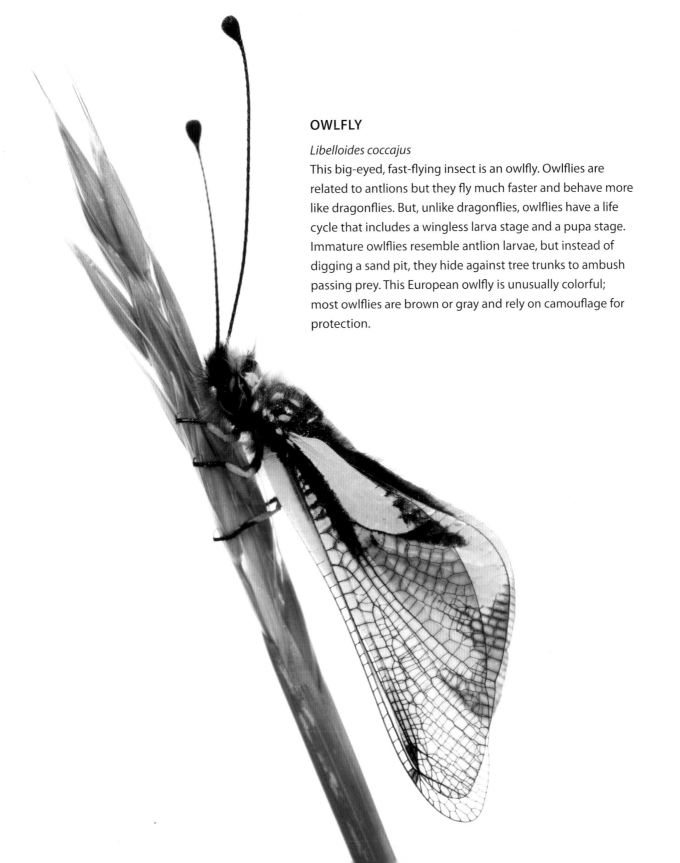

OWLFLY

Libelloides coccajus

This big-eyed, fast-flying insect is an owlfly. Owlflies are related to antlions but they fly much faster and behave more like dragonflies. But, unlike dragonflies, owlflies have a life cycle that includes a wingless larva stage and a pupa stage. Immature owlflies resemble antlion larvae, but instead of digging a sand pit, they hide against tree trunks to ambush passing prey. This European owlfly is unusually colorful; most owlflies are brown or gray and rely on camouflage for protection.

MAGPIE MOTH CATERPILLAR

Abraxas grossulariata

This magpie moth larva is a kind of "looper" or "inchworm." Caterpillars in this family (Geometridae) got their name because they inch along in a looping motion, as you can see here, rather than crawling forward using their legs like most other caterpillars. Like the caterpillar, the adult moth also has spots, on the body and wings. They have a very large range across Europe, Russia and North America.

BUCK MOTH CATERPILLAR

Hemileuca maia

This buck moth caterpillar, like many other caterpillars, is beautifully decorated with spikes and spines loaded with nasty defensive chemicals. Touching this kind of caterpillar can hurt and cause a bad rash. Buck moths are found on oak trees in eastern North America, where the adults emerge very late in the season. Unlike most moths, the black-and-white adults are active during the day. They fly very fast and are difficult to catch.

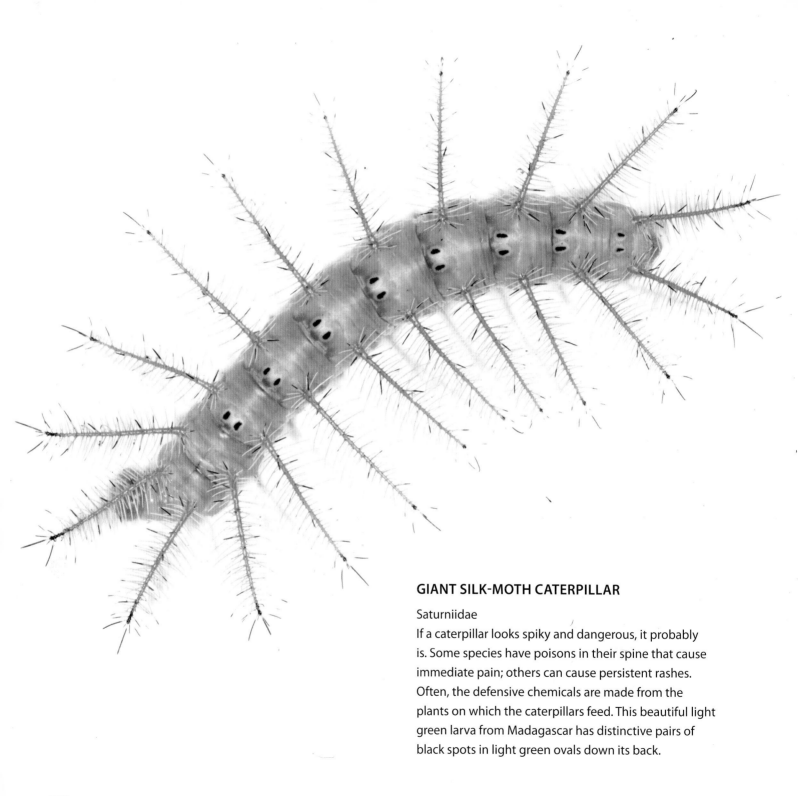

GIANT SILK-MOTH CATERPILLAR

Saturniidae

If a caterpillar looks spiky and dangerous, it probably is. Some species have poisons in their spine that cause immediate pain; others can cause persistent rashes. Often, the defensive chemicals are made from the plants on which the caterpillars feed. This beautiful light green larva from Madagascar has distinctive pairs of black spots in light green ovals down its back.

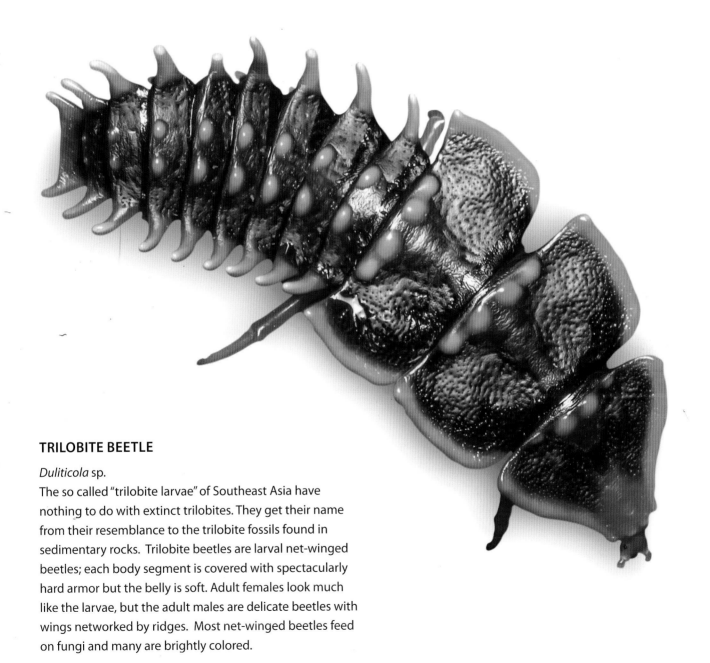

TRILOBITE BEETLE

Duliticola sp.

The so called "trilobite larvae" of Southeast Asia have nothing to do with extinct trilobites. They get their name from their resemblance to the trilobite fossils found in sedimentary rocks. Trilobite beetles are larval net-winged beetles; each body segment is covered with spectacularly hard armor but the belly is soft. Adult females look much like the larvae, but the adult males are delicate beetles with wings networked by ridges. Most net-winged beetles feed on fungi and many are brightly colored.

SCORPIONFLY

Panorpa nuptialis

Scorpionflies are harmless scavengers and predators unable to inflict any harm on humans. The scary sting-like tail that makes the fly resemble a scorpion is just the male genitalia. The scorpionfly belongs to the order Mecoptera, which means "long wings" in Greek and certainly describes this insect. The larva resembles a small caterpillar and the insects perform a valuable service as scavengers that clean up the environment.

CRANE FLY

Nephrotoma crocata

This is one of the more colorful of the 15,000 or so species of crane flies (Tipulidae) found around the world. You can tell it is a male by the branched antennae and stubby tip of the abdomen. The female lays eggs in the soil. When they hatch the larvae live by eating plant roots. Like all flies, the hind wings are reduced to little knobs, called halteres, clearly visible behind the left wing of the fly in this photograph.

DOBSONFLY

Chloronia mexicana
Adult *Chloronia* lack the long tusks found in males of the genus *Corydalus*. Also, *Chloronia* is more a tropical genus, whereas *Corydalus* is found as far north as Ontario, Canada.

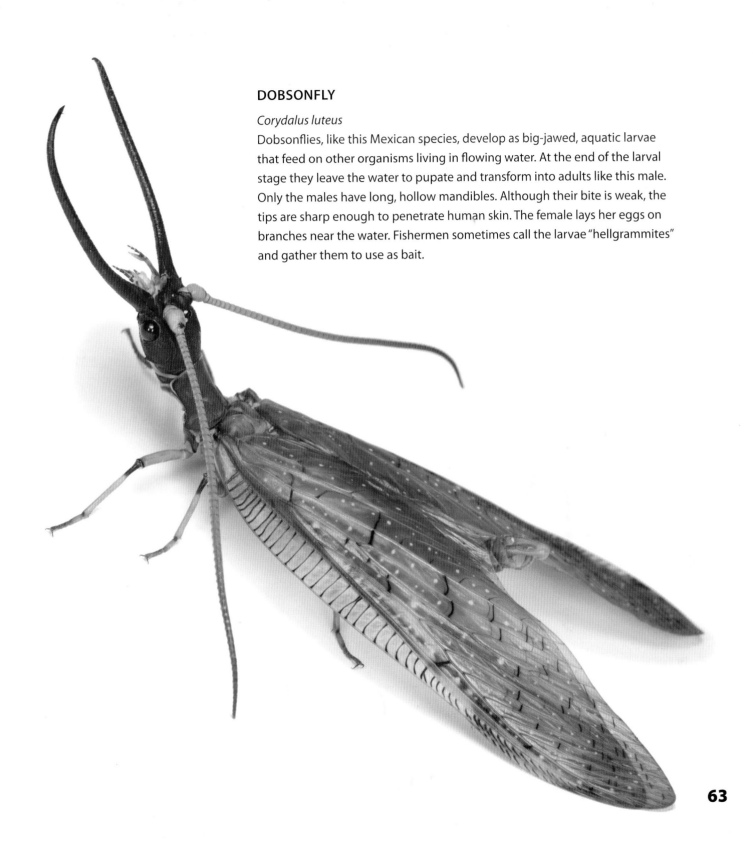

DOBSONFLY

Corydalus luteus

Dobsonflies, like this Mexican species, develop as big-jawed, aquatic larvae that feed on other organisms living in flowing water. At the end of the larval stage they leave the water to pupate and transform into adults like this male. Only the males have long, hollow mandibles. Although their bite is weak, the tips are sharp enough to penetrate human skin. The female lays her eggs on branches near the water. Fishermen sometimes call the larvae "hellgrammites" and gather them to use as bait.

INDEX